THE SPIRITUAL COUPLETS
OF
MAULANA JALALU-'D-DIN MUHAMMAD RUMI

Abridged and Translated

E.H. Whinfield

Masnavi
Book 3

[ZHINGOORA BOOKS]

STORY I.
The Travelers who ate the Young Elephant.

A PARTY of travelers lost their way in a wilderness, and were well nigh famished with hunger. While they were considering what to do, a sage came up and condoled with them on their unfortunate plight. He told them that there were many young elephants in the adjacent woods, one of which would furnish them an ample meal, but at the same time he warned them that if they killed one, its parents would in all probability track them out and be revenged on them for killing their offspring. Shortly after the travelers saw a plump young elephant, and could not resist killing and eating it. One alone refrained. Then they lay down to rest; but no sooner were they fast asleep than a huge elephant made his appearance and proceeded to smell the breath of each one of the sleepers in turn. Those whom he perceived to have eaten of the young elephant's flesh he slew without mercy, sparing only the one who had been prudent enough to abstain.

God's care for His children.

O son, the pious are God's children,
Absent or present He is informed of their state.
Deem Him not absent when they are endangered,
For He is jealous for their lives.
He saith, "These saints are my children,
Though remote and alone and away from their Lord.
For their trial they are orphans and wretched,
Yet in love I am ever holding communion with them.
Thou art backed by all my protection;
My children are, as it were, parts of me.
Verily these Darveshes of mine
Are thousands on thousands, and yet no more than One;
For if not, how did Moses with one magic staff

Turn the realm of Pharaoh upside down?
And if it were not so, how did Noah with one curse
Make East and West alike drowned in his flood?
Nor could one prayer of eloquent Lot
Have razed their strong city against their will,
Their mighty city, like to Paradise,
Became as a Tigris of black water; go, see its vestige!
Towards Syria is this vestige and memorial,
Thou seest it in passing on the way to Jerusalem.
Thousands of God-fearing prophets
In every age hold divine chastisements in hand.
Should I tell of them my limits would be exceeded,
And not hearts only but very hills would bleed."
Evil deeds give men's prayers an ill savour in Gods nostrils.
Thou art asleep, and the smell of that forbidden fruit
Ascends to the azure skies,
Ascends along with thy foul breath,
Till it overpowers heaven with stench;
Stench of pride, stench of lust, stench of greed.
All these stink like onions when a man speaks.
Though thou swearest, saying, "When have I eaten?
Have I not abstained from onions and garlic?"
The very breath of that oath tells tales,
As it strikes the nostrils of them that sit with thee.
So too prayers are made invalid by such stenches, 1
That crooked heart is betrayed by its speech.
The answer to that prayer is, "Be ye driven into hell," 2
The staff of repulsion is the reward of all deceit.
But, if thy speech be crooked and thy meaning straight,
Thy crookedness of words will be accepted of God.
That faithful Bilal, when he called to prayer,
Would devoutly cry, "Come hither, come hither!"
At last men said, "O Prophet, this call is not right,
This is wrong; now, what is thy intention?
O Prophet, and O ambassador of the Almighty,

3

Provide another Mu'azzin of better talent.
'Tis an error at the beginning of our divine worship
To utter the words, 'Come to the asylum!'" 3
The wrath of the Prophet boiled up, and he said
(Uttering one or two secrets from the fount of grace),
"O base ones, in God's sight the 'Ho!' of Bilal
Is better than a hundred 'Come hithers' and ejaculations.
Ah! excite not a tumult, lest I tell forth openly
Your secret thoughts from first to last.
If ye keep not your breath sweet in prayer,
Go, desire a prayer from the Brethren of Purity!"
For this cause spake God to Moses,
At the time he was asking aid in prayer,
"O Moses! desire protection of me
With a mouth that thou hast not sinned withal."
Moses answered, "I possess not such a mouth."
God said, "Call upon me with another mouth!
Act so that all thy mouths
By night and by day may be raising prayers.
When thou hast sinned with one mouth,
With thy other mouth cry, 'O Allah!'
Or else cleanse thy own mouth,
And make thy spirit alert and quick.
Calling on God is pure, and when purity approaches,
Impurity arises and takes its departure.
Contraries flee away from contraries;
When day dawns night takes flight.
When the pure name (of God) enters the mouth,
Neither does impurity nor that impure mouth remain!"
The man whose calling "O Allah" was equivalent
to God's answering him, "Here am I" 4.

That person one night was crying, "O Allah!"
That his mouth might be sweetened thereby,
And Satan said to him, "Be quiet, O austere one!
How long wilt thou babble, O man of many words?
No answer comes to thee from nigh the throne,
How long wilt thou cry 'Allah' with harsh face?"
That person was sad at heart and hung his head,
And then beheld Khizr present before him in a vision,
Who said to him, "Ah! thou hast ceased to call on God,
Wherefore repentest thou of calling upon Him?"
The man said, "The answer 'Here am I' came not,
Wherefore I fear that I am repulsed from the door."
Khizr replied to him, "God has given me this command;
Go to him and say, 'O much-tried one,
Did not I engage thee to do my service?
Did not I engage thee to call upon me?
That calling 'Allah' of thine was my 'Here am I,'
And that pain and longing and ardour of thine my
messenger;
Thy struggles and strivings for assistance
Were my attractions, and originated thy prayer.
Thy fear and thy love are the cove,rt of my mercy,
Each 'O Lord!' of thine contains many 'Here am I's."
The soul of fools is alien from this calling on God,
Because it is not their wont to cry, 'O Lord!'
On their mouths and hearts are locks and bonds, 5
That they may not cry to God in time of distress.
God gave Pharaoh abundance of riches and wealth,
So that he boasted that he was 'Lord Supreme.'
In the whole of his life he suffered no headache,
So that he never cried to God, wretch that he was.
God granted him the absolute dominion of the world,
But withheld from him pain and sorrow and cares;
Because pain and sorrow and loads of cares
Are the lot of God's friends in the world.

Pain is better than the dominion of the world,
So that thou mayest call on God in secret.
The cries of those free from pain are dull and cold,
The cries of the sorrowful come from the burning hearts."

*NOTES:

1. "Whoever eats garlic or onions must keep away from me or from the Masjid." (Mishkat ut Masabih, ii. 321).

2. Koran xxiii. 110: "He will say 'Be ye driven down into it, and address me not.'"

3. Rules for the call to prayer are given in Mishkat ul Masabih i. 141.

4. Or, "What dost thou require of me?"

5. Koran ii. 6.

STORY II.
The Villager who invited the Townsman to visit him.

A certain villager paid a visit to the town, and there received hospitality from one of the townsmen. At his departure the villager was profuse of thanks, and pressed the townsman to come and see him in his village, and bring his family with him. The townsman hesitated long before accepting his invitation, having doubts as to his sincerity, and remembering the Hadis, "Caution consists in suspecting others." 1 But after ten years' solicitation he at length yielded, and set off with his family to the village. On his arrival the villager shut the door in his face, saying that he did not know him, and the townsman had to pass five nights in the cold and rain. At last, exhausted with suffering, he implored the villager to give him shelter, promising to render service in return. The villager granted it on condition that he would protect his garden from the wolves. The townsman accepted this condition, and taking bow and arrows, proceeded to patrol the garden, but, owing to the rain and the darkness, and his own fears, ended by shooting the villager's pet ass in mistake for a wolf. The villager abused him roundly, saying that he himself would not have taken an ass for a wolf, even on the darkest night. The townsman replied, "If that be so, you are self-convicted of inhumanity, for you must have recognized me, your friend of ten years' standing, the moment I knocked at your door. As for me, I am ignorant of all but Allah, and, moreover, was unable to see in the darkness; and God has said, 'No criminality is imputed to the blind.'2 But your blindness in refusing to recognize me was willful, and your claims to humanity are thus proved to be false by the test to which you have been submitted."
Jesus healing the sick.

The house of 'Isa was the banquet of men of heart,
Ho! afflicted one, quit not this door!
From all sides the people ever thronged,
Many blind and lame, and halt and afflicted,
To the door of the house of 'Isa at dawn,
That with his breath he might heal their ailments.
As soon as he had finished his orisons,
That holy one would come forth at the third hour;
He viewed those impotent folk, troop by troop,
Sitting at his door in hope and expectation;
He spoke to them, saying, "O stricken ones!
The desires of all of you have been granted by God;
Arise, walk without pain or affliction,
Acknowledge the mercy and beneficence of God!"
Then all, as camels whose feet are shackled,
When you loose their feet in the road,
Straightway rush in joy and delight to the halting-place,
So did they run upon their feet at his command.
How many afflictions caused by thyself to thyself
Hast thou escaped through these princes of the faith?
How long that lameness of thine was thy steed!
How seldom was thy soul void of sorrow and grief!
O careless straggler, bind a rope upon thy feet,
Lest thou lose even thine own self!
But thy ingratitude and unthankfulness
Forget the honey draught thou hast sipped.
That road was perforce closed to thee
When thou didst wound the hearts of the men of heart.
Quick! clasp them and ask pardon of them;
Like the clouds, shed tears of lamentation,
So that their rose-garden may bloom for thee,
And their ripe fruits burst open of themselves.
Press around that door, be not viler than a dog,
If thou wouldest rival the Seven Sleepers' dog.
God's claims to our gratitude.

Whereas want of fidelity is shameful even in dogs,
How can it be right in men?
God Almighty Himself makes boast of fidelity,
Saying, "Who more faithful to his promise than We?" 3
Know, infidelity is fidelity to God's adversary,
No one has pre-eminence over the rights of God.
The claims of a mother are less than God's, for He,
That bounteous One, made her debtor for thy embryo.
He gave thee a form whilst thou wast in her womb,
In her womb He gave thee needful rest and nurture.
He viewed her as a part united to thee,
Then His wisdom separated that united part.
God devised a thousand plans and arts,
To make thy mother lavish affection upon thee.
Wherefore the claims of God predominate over the mother's,
Whoso acknowledges not God's claims is a fool.
He who made mother and breast and milk
United mother to father also, despise Him not!
O Lord, O Ancient of days, Thy mercies,
Whether known to us or unknown, are all from Thee!
Thou hast commanded, saying, "Remember thy God,"
Because God's claims are never exhausted!
Since thou hast been led astray by faithless men,
Turn now from thy evil doubts to the opposite mind.
I am free from error and all faithlessness;
Thou must come to me and rescind evil doubts.
Cut off these evil doubts and cast them away,
For in the presence of such thou becomest double.
Therefore thou hast chosen harsh friends and companions;
If I ask where they are thou sayest they are gone.
The good friend goes up to highest heaven,
Evil friends sink beneath the bottom of the earth,
Whilst thou art left alone in the midst, forlorn,
Even as the fires left by the departed caravan."
O brave friend, grasp His skirt,

9

Who is removed alike from the world above and below;
Who neither, like. Jesus, ascends to heaven,
Nor, like Korah, sinks into the earth;
Who will abide with thee in the house and abroad
When thou lackest house and home.
He will bring forth peace out of perturbations,
And when thou art afllicted will keep His promise.
How false pretensions to sanctity are
distinguished from true sanctity.
O son, a hundred thousand tests await thee,
Whoever thou art who sayest "I am a prince of the gate,"
If the vulgar detect not such an one by tests,
Yet the skilled wayfarers seek of him a sign.
When a man makes pretension to be a tailor,
The master places before him a piece of silk,
Saying, "Cut out a large head-dress,"
And failure in the test leads him to the pillory.
If all the evil men were not tested,
Every catamite would through fraud pass for a Rustam.
Suppose he wears the semblance of one clad in mail,
Yet when wounded he is at once taken captive.
The God-intoxicated are not sobered by old age,
They remain beside themselves till the last trump.
The wine of God is true, and not false,
But thou hast drunk only sour whey.
Thou makest thyself out to be a Junaid or a Bayazid;
Go! for do I not know a hatchet from a ploughshare?
O plotter, how canst thou conceal by fraud
Baseness, sloth, covetousness, and lust?
Thou holdest thyself out as a lover of God,
But thou hast coquetted with the evil demon.
The lover and the beloved on the last day
Will be joined together and raised in sight of all.
How foolish and silly thou hast made thyself!
Thou hast drunk blood of grapes, nay, my blood!

Go! for I know thee not. Get away!
I am a lover beside himself, whose words are wild.
Thou fanciest thyself near to God,
Saying, "The maker of the dish is not far from the dish."
Knowest thou not that the nearness of saints to God
Involves the power to do mighty works and signs?
Iron was as wax in the hands of David,
Wax in thy hands is as iron.
God's nearness and His beneficence are common to all,
But only eminent saints enjoy inspired love.
Nearness is of various kinds, O son,
The sun shines alike on rocks and on gold.
Yet the sun possesses a nearness to gold,
Whereof the common willow has no cognizance.
The dry branch and the green are alike near the sun,
Does the sun veil himself from either?
Yet what is the nearness of that green branch,
Wherefrom thou eatest ripe fruits?
But as for the dry branch) from its nearness to the sun,
What does it but more quickly grow dry and sapless?
Be not intoxicated after the manner of this branch,
Which, when it becomes sober, has cause for repentance,
But, like those drunkards who, when they drink wine,
Bear ripe fruits of wisdom of penitence.
*NOTES:
1. Freytag, Arabum Proverbia, i. p. 370, ascribes this saying to
the poet, Aqzam bin zaid.
2. Koran xxiv. 60.
3. Koran. ix. 112.

STORY III.
The Jackal who pretended to be a Peacock.

A jackal fell into a dye-pit, and his skin was dyed of various colors. Proud of his splendid appearance, he returned to his companions, and desired them to address him as a peacock. But they proceeded to test his pretensions, saying, "Dost thou scream like a peacock, or strut about gardens as peacocks are wont to do?" And he was forced to admit that he did not, whereupon they rejected his pretensions. Another story, also on the subject of false pretenders, follows. A proud man who lacked food procured a skin full of fat, greased his beard and lips with it, and called on his friends to observe how luxuriously he had dined. But his belly was vexed at this, because it was hungry, and he was destroying his chance of being invited to dinner by his friends. So the belly cried to God, and a cat came and carried off the skin of fat, and so the man's false pretences were exposed. The poet takes occasion to point out that Pharaoh's pretensions to divinity exactly resembled the pretensions of this jackal, and adds that all such false pretenders may be detected by the mark noted in the Koran, "Ye shall know them by the strangeness of their speech." 1 This recalls the story of Harut and Marut, two angels who were very severe on the frailties of mankind, and whom God sent down upon the earth to be tempted, with the result that they both succumbed to the charms of the daughters of men.2
*NOTES:
1. Koran xlvii. 32.
2. Koran ii. 96.

STORY IV.
Moses and Pharaoh.

Then follows a long account of the birth of Moses, of
Pharaoh's devices to kill him in his infancy, of his education in
Pharaoh's house, of his desiring Pharaoh to let the children of
Israel go, and of his contest with the magicians of Egypt, and
his victory over them. In the course of the story the following
anecdote is narrated:
A snake-catcher, who was following his occupation in the
mountains, discovered a large snake frozen by the cold, and,
imagining it to be dead, he tied it up and took it to Baghdad.
There all the idlers of the city flocked together to see it, and
the snake, thawed by the warmth of the sun, recovered life,
and immediately destroyed the spectators.
Comparison of fleshly lust to the snake.

Lust is that snake; How say you it is dead?
It is only frozen by the pangs of hunger.
If it obtains the state of Pharaoh,
So as to command the (frozen) rivers to flow,
Straightway it is led to pride like Pharaoh's,
And it plunders the goods of many a Moses and Aaron.
Through pressure of want this snake is as a fly,
It becomes a gnat through wealth and rank and luxury.
Beware, keep that snake in the frost of humiliation,
Draw it not forth into the sunshine of 'Iraq!
So long as that snake is frozen, it is well;
When it finds release from frost you become its prey.
Conquer it and save yourself from being conquered,
Pity it not, it is not one who bears affection.
For that warmth of the sun kindles its lust,

And that bat of vileness flaps its wings.
Slay it in sacred war and combat,
Like a valiant man will God requite you with union.
When that man cherished that snake,
That stubborn brute was happy in the luxury of warmth;
And of necessity worked destruction, O friend;
Yea, many more mischiefs than I have told.
If you wish to keep that snake tied up
Without trouble, be faithful, be faithful!
But how can base men attain this wish?
It requires a Moses to slay serpents;
And a hundred thousand men were slain by his serpent,
In dire confusion, according to his purpose.

STORY V.
The Elephant in a Dark Room.

Some Hindoos were exhibiting an elephant in a dark room,
and many people collected to see it. But as the place was too
dark to permit them to see the elephant, they all felt it with
their hands, to gain an idea of what it was like. One felt its
trunk, and declared that the beast resembled a water-pipe;
another felt its ear, and said it must be a large fan; another its
leg, and thought it must be a pillar; another felt its back, and
declared the beast must be like a great throne. According to
the part which each felt, he gave a different description of the
animal. One, as it were, called it "Dal" and another "Alif."
Comparison of the sensual eye to the
hand of one that felt the elephant.
The eye of outward sense is as the palm of a hand,
The whole of the object is not grasped in the palm.
The sea itself is one thing, the foam another;
Neglect the foam, and regard the sea with your eyes.
Waves of foam rise from the sea night and day,
You look at the foam ripples and not the mighty sea.
We, like boats, are tossed hither and thither,
We are blind though we are on the bright ocean.
Ah! you who are asleep in the boat of the body,
You see the water; behold the Water of waters!
Under the water you see there is another Water moving it,
Within the spirit is a Spirit that calls it.
Where were Moses and Jesus when that Sun
Showered down water on the fields sown with corn?
Where were Adam and Eve what time
God Almighty fitted the string to His bow?
The one form of speech is evil and defective;
The other form, which is not defective, is perfect.

If I speak thereof your feet stumble,
Yet if I speak not of it, woe be to you!
And if I speak in terms of outward form,
You stick fast in that same form, O son.
You are footbound like the grass in the ground,
And your head is shaken by the wind uncertainly.
Your foot stands not firmly till you move it,
Nay) till you pluck it not up from the mire.
When you pluck up your foot you escape from the mire,
The way to this salvation is very difficult.
When you obtain salvation at God's hands, O wanderer,
You are free from the mire, and go your way.
When the suckling is weaned from its nurse,
It eats strong meats and leaves the nurse.
You are bound to the bosom of earth like seeds,
Strive to be weaned through nutriment of the heart.
Eat the words of wisdom, for veiled light
Is not accepted in preference to unveiled light.
When you have accepted the light, O beloved,
When you behold what is veiled without a veil,
Like a star you will walk upon the heavens;
Nay, though not in heaven, you will walk on high.
Keep silence, that you may hear Him speaking
Words unutterable by tongue in speech.
Keep silence, that you may hear from that Sun
Things inexpressible in books and discourses.
Keep silence, that the Spirit may speak to you;
Give up swimming and enter the ark of Noah;
Not like Canaan when he was swimming,
Who said, "I desire not to enter the ark of Noah passing by."
Noah and his unbelieving son Canaan.
Noah cried, "Ho! child, come into the ark and rest,
That you be not drowned in the flood, O weak one." 1
Canaan said, "Nay! I have learned to swim,
I have lit a torch of my own apart from thy torch."

Noah replied, "Make not light of it, for 'tis the flood of
destruction,
Swimming with hands and feet avails naught today.
The wind of wrath and the storm blow out torches;
Except the torch of God, all are extinguished."
He answered "Nay! I am going to that high mountain,
For that will save me from all harm."
Noah cried, "Beware, do not so, mountains are now as grass;
Except the Friend none can save thee."
He answered, "Why should I listen to thy advice?
For thou desirest to make me one of thy flock.
Thy speech is by no means pleasing to me,
I am free from thee in this world and the next."
Thus the more good advice Noah gave him,
The more stubborn refusals he returned.
Neither was his father tired of advising Canaan,
Nor did his advice make any impression on Canaan;
While they were yet talking a violent wave
Smote Canaan's head, and he was overwhelmed.
Reconciliatian of the two traditions, "Acquiescence in
infidelity is infidelity" and "Whoso acquiesces not in God's
ordinance desires another Lord besides me".
Yesterday an inquirer questioned me,
Since he was interested in the foregoing narrative,
Saying, "The Prophet, whose words are as a seal,
Said, 'Acquiescence in infidelity is infidelity.'
And again, 'Acquiescence in God's ordinance
Is incumbent on all true believers.'
Infidelity and hypocrisy are not ordained of God;
If I acquiesce in them I am at variance with God.
And yet, if I acquiesce not, that again is wrong;
What way of escape is there from this dilemma? "
I said to him, "This infidelity is ordained, not ordinance, 2
Though this infidelity is the work of the ordinance.
Therefore distinguish the ordinance from the ordained,

That thy difficulty may be at once removed.
I acquiesce in infidelity so far as it is God's ordinance,
Not so far as it is our evil and foul passions.
Infidelity qua ordinance is not infidelity,
Call not God an infidel. Set not foot in this place.
Infidelity is folly, ordained infidelity wisdom,
How can mercy and vengeance be the same?
Ugliness of the picture is not ugliness of the painter,
Not so, for he erases ugly pictures.
The ability of the painter is shown in this,
That he can paint both ugly and beautiful pictures.
If I should pursue this argument properly,
So that questions and answers should be prolonged,
The unction of the mystery of love would escape me,
The picture of obedience would become another picture."
Bewilderment from intense love of God puts
an end to all thinking and argument 3.
A certain man whose hair was half gray came in haste
To a barber who was a friend of his,
Saying, "Pluck out the white hairs from my beard,
For I have selected a young bride, O my son.
The barber cut off his beard and laid it before him,
Saying, "Do you part them, the task is beyond me."
Questions are white and answers black; do you choose,
For the man of faith knows not how to choose.
Thus, one smote Zaid a blow,
And Zaid attacked him for his treachery.
The striker said, "Let me first ask you a question,
Give me an answer to it and then strike me;
I struck your back and a bruise appeared,
Now I ask you a question in all kindliness,
Did this bruise proceed from my hand,
Or from the smitten part of your back, O complainer?"
Zaid replied, "Through pain I am not in a condition
To enter upon thought and consideration of this.

You, who are free from pain, think this out;
Such trifling thoughts occur not to a man in pain."
Men in pain have no time for other thoughts,
Whether you enter mosque or Christian church.
Your carelessness and injustice suggest thoughts
And unprecedented difficulties to your imagination.
The man in pain cares only for the faith,
He is aware only of man and his work.
He set's God's command upon his head and face,
And for thinking, he puts it aside. 4

*NOTES:

1. Koran xi. 44.

2. Or "decreed, not decree" (maqzi nai qaza). I confess I do not understand the distinction.

3. See Gulshan i Raz, I. 287.

4. The four last couplets are omitted in the Bulaq edition.

STORY VI.
The Lover who read Sonnets to his Mistress.

A lover was once admitted to the presence of his mistress, but,
instead of embracing her, he pulled out a paper of sonnets
and read them to her, describing her perfections and charms
and his own love towards her at length. His mistress said to
him, "You are now in my presence, and these lover's sighs
and invocations are a waste of time. It is not the part of a true
lover to waste his time in this way. It shows that I am not the
real object of your affection, but that what you really love is
your own effusions and ecstatic raptures. I see, as it were, the
water which I have longed for before me, and yet you
withhold it. I am, as it were, in Bulgaria, and the object of your
love is in Cathay. One who is really loved is the single object
of her lover, the Alpha and Omega of his desires. As for you,
you are wrapped up in your own amorous raptures,
depending on the varying states of your own feelings, instead
of being wrapped up in me."
The true mystic must not stop at mere subjective religious
emotions, but seek absolute union with God. 1
Whoso is restricted to religious raptures is but a man;
Sometimes his rapture is excessive, sometimes deficient.
The Sufi is, as it were, the "son of the season,"
But the pure (Safi) is exalted above season and state.
Religious raptures depend on feelings and will,
But the pure one is regenerated by the breath of Jesus.
You are a lover of your own raptures, not of me;
You turn to me only in hope of experiencing raptures.
Whoso is now defective, now perfect,
Is not adored by Abraham; he is "one that sets."

Because the stars set, and are now up, now down,
He loved them not; "I love not them that set." 2
Whoso is now pleasing and now unpleasing
Is at one time water, at another fire.
He may be the house of the moon, but not the true moon;
Or as the picture of a mistress, but not the living one.
The mere Sufi is the " child of the season;"
He clings to seasons as to a father,
But the pure one is drowned in overwhelming love.
A child of any one is never free from season and state.
The pure one is drowned in the light cc that is not begotten,"
"What begets not and is not begotten" is God. 3
Go I seek such love as this, if you are alive;
If not, you are enslaved by varying seasons.
Gaze not on your own pictures, fair or ugly,
Gaze on your love and the object of your desire.
Gaze not at the sight of your own weakness or vileness,
Gaze at object of your desire, O exalted one.
*NOTES:
1. See Gulshan i Raz, I. 850.
2. Koran vi. 77.
3. Koran cxii. 3.

STORY VII.

The Man who prayed earnestly to be fed without work.
In the time of the prophet David there was a man who used to
pray day and night, saying, "Thou hast created me weak and
helpless; give me my daily bread without obliging me to work
for it." The people derided him for making such a foolish
petition, but he still persisted, and at last a cow ran into his
house of its own accord, and he killed and ate it. This
illustrates the saying of the Prophet that God loves earnest
petitioners, because He regards the sincerity of the prayer
more than the nature of the thing prayed for. All things praise
God, but the praises of inanimate things are different from the
praises of men, and those of a Sunni different from those of a
Compulsionist (Jabri). Each says the other is in the way of
error, but none but the truly spiritual man knows the truth.
Knowledge or conviction, opposed to opinion.
Little is known by any one but the spiritual man,
Who has in his heart a touchstone of vital truth.
The others, hovering between two opinions,
Fly towards their nest on a single wing.
Knowledge has two wings, opinion only one wing;
Opinion is weak and lopsided in its flight.
The bird having but one wing quickly drops down,
And again flies on two steps or more.
This bird of opinion goes on rising and falling
On one wing, in hope to reach his nest.
When he escapes from opinion and knowledge is seen,
This bird gains two wings and spreads both of them.
Afterwards he "goes upright on a straight path,
Not grovelling on his face or creeping." 1
He flies up on two wings even as the angel Gabriel,
Free of opinion, of duplicity, and of vain talk.

Though the whole world say to him,
"Thou art firm in the road of God's faith,"
He is not made more ardent by their saying this,
Nor is his lofty soul inclined from its course.
And though all say to him, "Thou art in the wrong way
Thou thinkest thyself a rock who art but a blade of grass,"
He relapses not into opinion at their rebukes,
Nor is he vexed at their malevolence.
Nay, even if sea and mountains should cry out,
Saying, "Thou art mated with error,"
He would not relapse one jot into vain imaginations,
Nor would he be grieved by the reproaches of his foes.
*NOTES:
1. Koran lxvii, 22.

STORY VIII.
The Boys and their Teacher.

To illustrate the force of imagination or opinion, a story is told of a trick played by boys upon their master. The boys wished to obtain a holiday, and the sharpest of them suggested that when the master came into the school each boy should condole with him on his alleged sickly appearance. Accordingly, when he entered, one said, "O master, how pale you are looking!" and another said, "You are looking very ill today," and so on. The master at first answered that there was nothing the matter with him, but as one boy after another continued assuring him that he looked very ill, he was at length deluded into imagining that he must really be ill. So he returned to his house, making the boys follow him there, and told his wife that he was not well, bidding her mark how pale he was. His wife assured him he was not looking pale, and offered to convince him by bringing a mirror; but he refused to look at it, and took to his bed. He then ordered the boys to begin their lessons; but they assured him that the noise made his head ache, and he believed them, and dismissed them to their homes, to the annoyance of their mothers. Apropos of the sharpness of the boy who devised this trick, the poet takes occasion to controvert the opinion of the Mu'tazalites, that all m en are born with equal ability, and to express his agreement with the doctrine of the Sunnis, that the innate capacities of men vary very greatly.

STORY IX.
The Darvesh who Broke his Vow.

There was once a Darvesh who took up his abode in the mountains, in order to enjoy perfect solitude. In that place were many fruit-trees, and the Darvesh made a vow that he would never pluck any of the fruit, but eat only what was shaken down by the wind. For a long time he kept his vow; but a time came when there was no wind, and consequently no fruit was shaken down. The Darvesh was true to his vow for five days, but ho could then endure the pangs of hunger no longer, and he stretched out his hand and plucked some of the fruit from the branches. The reason of this lapse on his part was that he had omitted to say "If God will" when making his vow; and as nothing can be accomplished without God's aid, ho could not possibly keep his vow. Shortly afterwards the chief of the police visited the mountains in pursuit of a band of robbers, and arrested the Darvesh along with them, and cut off his hand. When he discovered his mistake he apologized very earnestly; but the Darvesh reassured him, saying that men were not to blame, as God had evidently designed to punish him for breaking his vow 'by depriving him of the hand which had sinned in plucking the fruit. 1
All things dependent upon the will of God.

Therefore hath God commanded, "Make an exception,
Couple the words 'If God will' with your vows. 2
Because the governance of actions is in my hands,
The wills of all are subject to my will.

Every moment I impart a fresh bias to the heart,
Every instant I set a fresh mark on the heart;
Each day I am engaged in a fresh work, 3
There is naught that swerves from my purpose."
There is a tradition, "The heart is like a feather
In the desert, which is borne captive by the winds; 4
The wind drives it everywhere at random,
Now to right and now to left in opposite directions."
According to another tradition, know the heart is like
To water in a kettle boiling on the fire.
So every moment a fresh purpose occurs to the heart,
Not proceeding from itself, but from its situation.
Why, then, are you confident about the heart's purposes?
Why make you vows only to be covered with shame?
All these changes proceed from the effect of God's will;
Although you see the pit, you cannot avoid it.
The strange thing is, not that winged fowl
Fall into the deadly snare without seeing it,
But that they see the snare and the limed twig,
And yet fall into it, whether they will or no;
Their eyes and ears are open and the snare is in front,
Yet they fly into the snare with their own wings!
Comparison of the divine decrees to something
that is hidden, yet whose effects are seen.
Behold that king's son clad in rags,
With bare head and fallen into distress;
Consumed by lusts and riotous living,
Having sold all his clothes and substance;
Having lost house and home, utterly disgraced,
Fulfilling the desire of his enemies by his disgrace.
If he sees a pious man he cries, "O sir,
Aid me, for the love of God;
For I have fallen into this dire disgrace;
I have squandered goods and gold and wealth.
Aid me so that perchance I may escape hence,

And extricate myself from this deep slough."
He repeats this prayer to high and low,
" Release me, release me, release me!"
His eyes and ears are open, and he is free from bonds,
No jailer watches him, no chain binds him;
What, then, is the bond from which he asks release?
What is the prison from which ho seeks an exit?
'Tis the bond of God's purpose and hidden decrees;
Ah! none but the pure in sight can see that bond;
Though not visible, that bond exists in concealment;
'Tis more stringent than prison or chains of iron,
For the mason can pull down prison walls,
And blacksmiths can break asunder iron chains;
But, strange to say, this ponderous hidden bond,
Blacksmiths are impotent to break this asunder!
Ahmad alone could see that bond on Omm Jahil's back, 5
And the rope of palm fiber bound upon her neck;
Yea, he saw wood on the back of the wife of Bu Lahab,
And she, the bearer of the firewood, said it was heavy.
No eye but his saw that rope and that firewood,
For to him things unseen were visible.
The others explained it, saying
That Ahmad was beside himself, and they in their senses.
Nevertheless from the weight of the load her back bent,
And she complained of its weight before him,
Saying, "Aid me to escape from this load,
And to shake off this grievous burden."
He who sees clearly these indications,
Does he not know also the doomed from the elect?
Yea, he knows them, yet conceals it by command of God,
Since God permits him not to reveal it.
*NOTES:
1. cp. Cranmer.
2. Koran xviii. 23.
3. Koran lv. 29; cp. John v. 17.

4. Freytag, Arabum Proverbia, vol. iii. p. 490.
5. See Koran cxi.: Abu Labab, at the instigation of his wife, Omm Jahil, rejected Muhammad's claim to the prophetic office and Muhammad declared that they should be burned in the fiery flame," and the wife "laden with firewood, and on her neck a rope of palm fiber."

STORY X.
The Old Man who made no Lamentation at the Death of his Sons.

After short anecdotes of Pharaoh's magicians, of the mule who complained to the camel that he was always stumbling, and of the prophet Ezra, comes the story of the old man who wept not for the death of his sons.
An old man who was noted for sanctity, and who realized the saying of the Prophet, "The 'ulama of the faith are as the prophets of Israel," lost all his sons, but showed no grief or regret. His wife therefore rebuked him for his want of feeling, whereupon he replied to her as follows:
He turned to his wife and said, "O dame,
The harvest of December is not as that of July;
Though they be dead or though they be living,
Are they not equally visible to the eyes of the heart?
I behold them clearly before me,
Wherefore should I disfigure my countenance like you?
Though they have gone forth by revolution of fortune,
They are with me still, playing round me.
The cause of lamentation is separation or parting,
But I am still with my dear ones, and embrace them.
Ordinary people may see them in dreams,
But I see them clearly, though wide awake.
I conceal myself a while from this world,
I shake down the leaves of outward sense from the tree.
Know, O wife, outward sense is captive to reason,
And reason, again, is captive to spirit.
Spirit unlooses the chained hands of reason;
Yea, it opens all things that are closed.
Sensations and thoughts resemble weeds
Which occupy the surface of pure water.
The hand of reason puts these weeds aside,

And the pure water is then visible to the wise.
Weeds in plenty cover the stream like bubbles;
When they are swept aside, the water is seen;
But when God unlooses not the hands of reason,
The weeds on our water grow thick through carnal lust;
Yea, they cover up your water more and more,
While your lust is smiling and your reason weeping.
When fear of God binds the hands of lust,
Then God unlooses the two hands of reason.
Then the powerful senses are subdued by you,
When you submit to reason as your commander
Then your sleepless sense is lulled into sleep,
That mysteries may appear to the soul.
You behold visions when broad awake,
And the gates of heaven are open before you."

STORY XI.
Bahlol and the Darvesh.

The foregoing story is followed by anecdotes of a blind saint
who was miraculously enabled to read the Koran, of Luqman
and David, and a description of the saints who, mindful of the
saying, "Patience is the key of happiness, resign themselves to
the dispensations of Providence, and never pray to have them
altered. The story of Bahlol and the Darvesh is then given as
an example of this resignation to the will of God. Bahlol once
paid a visit to a saintly Darvesh, and asked him how he fared.
The Darvesh replied, "I fare like a man who directs the course
of the world as he wills, to whom death and life are
subservient, and whom tho stars themselves obey." Bahlol
then pressed him to explain his meaning more clearly, and the
Darvesh replied as follows:
He said, "This at least is notorious to all men,
That the world obeys the command of God.
Not a leaf falls from a tree
Without the decree and command of that Lord of lords;
Not a morsel goes from the mouth down the throat
Till God says to it, 'Go down.'
Desire and appetite, which are the reins of mankind,
Are themselves subservient to the rule of God.
Hear this much, that, whereas the totality of actions
Is not effected without God's direction,
When the decree of God becomes the pleasure of man,
Then man desires the fulfillment of God's decrees;
And this too spontaneously, not in hope of reward,
But because his very nature is congruous therewith.
He desires not even his own life for himself,
Nor is he relying on the hope of sweets of life to come.
Whatever path is taken by the eternal decree,
Whether it be life or death, 'tis all one to him.

He lives for the sake of God, not for wealth;
He dies for the sake of God, not in fear and grief.
His faith is based on his desire to do God's will,
Not on hope to gain paradise with its groves and founts.
His avoidance of infidelity is also for God's sake,
It proceeds not from fear of falling into the fire.
Thus this temper of his arises from his very nature,
Not from any discipline and endeavor of his own.
At times he laughs when he contemplates God's pleasure,
God's decrees are to him as sweetmeats of sugar.
I ask, does not the world march agreeably to the will
And commands of a man rejoicing in this disposition?
Why, then, should such a one make prayers and petitions,
Saying, 'O God, change such and such a decree?'
His own death and his children's deaths
For God's sake seem to him as sweets in the mouth.
In the view of that faithful one his children's deaths
Are as sweetmeats to a starving beggar.
Why, therefore, should he make prayers
Unless he pray for what is pleasing to God?
These prayers and petitions, not those of self-pity
Make that man to be endued with salvation.
He utterly burned up all his self-pity,
At the time when he lit the lamp of love to God.
His love was the hell that burned up his inclinations;
Yea, ho burned up his own inclinations one by one."

STORY XII.
The Visions seen by the Saint Daquqi.

To illustrate the exalted state of identification of the will with the Divine will just described, the poet tells the story of the visions and mighty works of the holy Daquqi. Daquqi was journeying in pious fervor, and in hope to see the splendour of "The Friend" in human shape, the Ocean in a drop of water, and the Sun in an atom, when late one evening he arrived at the seashore. Turning his eyes to heaven, he saw seven great lights never before seen of men, for "God directs whom He will." 1 Overwhelmed with awe, he watched these lights, and while he still watched them they united into one light. Still more amazed, he watched on, and the single light shortly assumed the likeness of seven men. Afterwards these seven men changed into seven trees; but, strange to say, although crowds of people were passing by, none of them could see these trees, so that Daquqi shared the feelings of the apostles "who lost all hope" (of convincing the world), "and deemed that, they were reckoned as liars." 2 Possessing his soul in patience, Daquqi still watched on, and saw the seven trees bowing down in prayer, and was reminded of the text, "Plants and trees bend in adoration." 3 Presently the seven trees again changed into seven men, and Daquqi was appointed to conduct their devotions. While he was yet acting as Imam in front of them, and they were following the prayers he recited, a ship was seen in great distress and all but lost. At Daquqi's earnest prayer the crew were saved, but straightway vanished from sight; and this led his followers to doubt the reality of the miracle which had just been performed before their eyes. Description of a saint whose will was identified with God's will.

That Daquqi possessed a sweet aspect,

As a lover of God and a worker of miracles.
He resembled the moon of heaven come down on earth,
He was as a light to them that walked in darkness.
He rarely tarried in one place,
And seldom stayed two days in one village.
He said, "If I tarry in one house two days,
Attachment to that house becomes a passion with me.
I guard myself from being deceived into loving a home;
Up! Soul, and travel in search of eternal wealth.
My heart's inclination is not satisfied by houses,
So that they should be places of temptation for me."
Thus by day he traveled, and by night prayed,
His eyes were always gazing on the King as a falcon's;
Cut off from mankind, though not for any fault,
Severed from men and women, though not for baseness;
Having compassion on mankind, and wholesome as water,
A kind intercessor, and one whose prayers were heard.
Benevolent to the good and the bad, and a firm ally,
Better than a mother, and kinder than a father.
The Prophet said, "To you, O blessed ones,
I am as a father, affectionate and indulgent;
For this cause, that you are all portions of me."
Wherefore should you tear away the parts from the whole?
If the part be severed from its whole it is useless;
If a limb be rent from the body it dies.
Till it is again joined to its whole,
'Tis a dead thing, and a stranger to life.
Thus Daquqi, in devotions and praises and prayers,
Was ever seeking the particular favorites of God.
Throughout his long journeys his object was this,
To interchange a word with the favorites of God.
He cried continually as he went his way,
"O Lord, let me draw near to Thy chosen ones!"
So Daquqi (the mercy of God be upon him!)
Said, "I journeyed long time to East and to West,

I journeyed years and months for love of that Moon,
Heedless of the way, absorbed in God.
With bare feet I trod upon thorns and flints,
Seeing I was bewildered, and beside myself, and senseless.
Think not my feet touched the earth,
For the lover verily travels with the heart.
What knows the heart of road and stages?
What of distant and near, while it is drunk with love?
Distance and nearness are attributes of bodies,
The journeys of spirits are after another sort.
You journeyed from the embryo state to rationality
Without footsteps or stages or change of place,
The journey of the soul involves not time and place.
And my body learnt from the soul its mode of journeying,
Now my body has renounced the bodily mode of journeying;
It journeys secretly and without form, though under a form."
He added, "One day I was thus filled with longing
To behold in human form the splendours of 'The Friend,'
To witness the Ocean gathered up into a drop,
The Sun compressed into a single atom;
And when I drew near to the shore of the sea
The day was drawing to a close."
All religions are in substance one and the same.
In the adorations and benedictions of righteous men
The praises of all the prophets are kneaded together.
All their praises are mingled into one stream,
All the vessels are emptied into one ewer.
Because He that is praised is, in fact, only One,
In this respect all religions are only one religion.
Because all praises are directed towards God's light,
Their various forms and figures are borrowed from it.
Men never address praises but to One deemed worthy,
They err only through mistaken opinions of Him.
So, when a light falls upon a wall,
That wall is a connecting-link between all its beams;

Yet when it casts that reflection back to its source,
It wrongly shows great as small, and halts in its praises.
Or if the moon be reflected in a well,
And one looks down the well, and mistakenly praises it,
In reality he is intending to praise the moon,
Although, through ignorance, he is looking down the well.
The object of his praises is the moon, not its reflection;
His infidelity arises from mistake of the circumstances.
That well-meaning man goes wrong through his mistake;
The moon is in heaven, and he fancies it in the well.
By these false idols mankind are perplexed,
And driven by vain lusts to their sorrow.
The Man in the time of the Prophet David who prayed
to be fed without having to work for his food.

After the petitioner had slain and eaten the cow, the owner of
the cow came up and accused him of theft, and seizing him by
the collar, dragged him before the judgment-seat of the
prophet David. When he had stated his case, David ordered
the accused to make restitution, telling him that he must not
break the law. At this order the accused redoubled his cries,
telling David that he was siding with an oppressor. David
was staggered at the man's assurance, and finally resolved to
take further time for consideration before deciding the case.
After private meditation he re-versed his former sentence, and
directed the plaintiff to relinquish his claim. On the plaintiff
refusing to do this, and stoutly protesting against David's
injustice. David further ordered that all the plaintiff's goods
should be given to the accused. The reason for this decision
was, that David discovered the plaintiff had formerly slain the
grandfather of the accused, and stolen all his goods. David
then led all the Mosalmans to a tree in the desert where the
murder had been perpetrated, and there put the murderer to
death.

The hands and feet of criminals betray
their crimes even in this world.
He of himself lifted the veil that hid his crime;
Had he not done so, God would have kept it hidden.
Criminals and sinners, even in the course of sinning,
Themselves rend the coverings of their crimes.
Their sins are veiled among the heart's secrets,
Yet the criminal himself exposes them to view,
Saying, "Behold me wearing a pair of horns,
A cow of hell in sight of all men."
Thus, even here, in the midst of thy sin, thy hand and foot
Bear witness of the secrets of thy heart.
Thy secret thought is as a governor who says to thee,
"Tell forth thy convictions, withhold them not;"
Especially in seasons of passion and angry talk
It betrays thy secrets one by one.
Thy secret sins and crimes govern hand and foot,
Saying, "Disclose us to men, O hand and foot!"
And since these witnesses take the bit in their mouths,
Especially in times of passion and wrath and revenge,
Therefore the same God who appointed this governor
To blazen forth thy secret sins to the world
Is also able to create many more governors
To divulge thy secret sins on the day of judgment. 4
O man whose only handiwork is crime and sin;
Thy secret sins are manifest; no divulging is needed.
There is no need to proclaim thy sins,
All men are cognizant of thy sin-burnt heart.
Thy soul every moment casts up sparks of fire,
Which say, "See me a man destined to the fire;
I am a part of the fire, and go to join my whole;
Not a light, so that I should join the Source of light."
Comparison of lust to the murderer in the story.
Kill thine own lust and give life to the world;
It has killed its lord, reduce it to servitude.

That claimant of the cow is thy lust; Beware!
It has made itself lord and master.
That slayer of the cow is thy reason; Go!
Be not obdurate to the prayers of him that kills the cow.
Reason is a poor captive, and ever cries to God
For meat on its dish without laboring and toiling.
On what depends its getting meat without toiling?
On its killing the cow of the body, the source of evil.
Lust says, "Why hast thou killed my cow?"
It says, "Because lust's cow is the form of the body." 5
Reason, the Lord's child, has become a pauper,
Lust, the murderer, has become a lord and chief.
Know'st thou what is meat untoiled for?
'Tis the food of spirits and the aliment of the Prophet.
But it is attainable only by slaying the cow;
Treasure is gained by digging, O digger of treasure!
*NOTES:
1. Koran lv. 5.
2. Koran xii. 110.
3. Koran ii. 136.
4. "On that day shall their hands speak unto us, and their feet
shall bear witness of that which they have done" (Koran
xxxvi. 65).
5. Bahau-'d-Din Amili, in his Nan wa Halwa, chap. iv.,
compares lust to a cow, referring to Koran ii. 63.

STORY XIII.
The People of Saba.

After an anecdote of 'Isa being obliged to ascend a mountain
to get away from the fools comes the story of the men of Saba.
"A sign there was to Saba in their dwelling-places two
gardens, the one on the right hand and the other on the left;
'Eat ye of your Lord's supplies, and give thanks to Him;
goodly is the country and gracious is the Lord.' But they
turned aside, so we sent upon them the flood of Iram. Such
was our retribution on them for their ingratitude." 1 The men
of Saba were all fools, and brought destruction on themselves
by their ingratitude to God. One was far-sighted, and yet
blind; another sharp of hearing, and yet deaf; and a third
naked, and yet wearing a long robe. Avarice is blind to its
own faults, but sees those of others; the sharp-eared deaf man
hears death approaching others, but not himself, and the long-
robed naked man is he who fears robbers, though he has
nothing to lose. In fact, all these men of Saba were afflicted
with follies and self-delusions of this kind, and gave no
thanks to God for the blessings which they enjoyed.
Accordingly thirteen prophets were sent to admonish them,
but their admonitions were not listened to, the men of Saba
questioning their divine mission and demanding a miracle as
a sign. They also told the prophets a parable of a clever hare,
who, wishing to frighten an elephant away from a fountain,
went to the elephant, pretending to be an ambassador from
the moon.2 The prophets were naturally indignant at the
effrontery of the men of Saba in misapplying parables to
discredit their divine mission, and reminded them that
wicked men had flouted the prophet Noah in the same way

39

when he was warning them of the flood. And they demonstrated at length how the men of Saba had misapplied the parable of the hare and the elephant, and again adjured them to believe. But the men of Saba continued refractory, and would not, accept the Prophets' counsels. They plied the prophets with the arguments of the Compulsionists (Jabriyan), and refused to be convinced of the fallacy of their reasoning. So at last the prophets despaired of them, and left them to their doom.

Not every one can properly use similitudes and parables in divine matters.

The faculty of using similitudes is peculiar to a saint
Who is signally marked by knowledge of hidden mysteries.
What know you of the mystery hid in aught, that you
In your folly should use similitudes of curl and cheek?
Moses took his staff to be a stick, though it was not;
It was a serpent, and its mystery was revealed.
If a saint such as he knew not the mystery of a stick,
What know you of the mystery of the snare and grains?
When the eye of a Moses erred as to a similitude,
How can a presumptuous mouse understand one?
Those similitudes of yours are changed into serpents
To tear you into pieces with their jaws.
Such a parable did cursed Iblis use,
So that he became cursed of God till the day of doom.
Such a parable did Korah use in his argument,
So that he was swallowed up in the earth with his wealth.
Such parables know to be as crows and owls,
Whereby a hundred households are annihilated.
When Noah was building the ark in the desert,
A hundred parable-mongers attacked him with irony,
Saying, "In the desert, where is no water or well,
He builds a boat! What ignorant folly is this!"
The arguments of the Jabriyan, i.e., the Fatalists or Compulsionists.

The men of Saba said, "O preachers, enough!
What you say is enough, if there are any wise here.
God has placed a 'lock upon our hearts,' 3
And no man can overcome the Creator.
That great Painter has painted us thus;
His painting cannot be altered by argument.
Keep telling forever a stone to become a ruby,
Keep telling forever the old to become young!
Tell earth to assume the quality of water,
Bid water to become honey or milk!
God is the creator of heaven and them that dwell therein;
Also of water and of earth, and them that dwell therein;
To heaven He gave its revolutions and its purity,
To the earth its dark look and appearance.
Can the heaven will to become as dregs?
Can earth will to assume the clearness of pure wine?
That Person has assigned 'to each its lot,
Can mountain by endeavor become as grass?"
The prophets answered, "Verily God has created
Some qualities in you which you cannot alter;
But He has created other accidental qualities,
Which, being objectionable, may be made good.
Bid stone become gold that is impossible;
Bid copper become gold that is possible.
Bid sand bloom as a rose it cannot;
Bid dust turn to mud that is within its capacity.
God has sent some pains for which there is no cure,
Such, for instance, as lameness, loss of nose, and blindness.
God has sent other pains for which there are cures,
To wit, crooked mouth and headache.
God has ordained these remedies of His mercy;
The use of these in pain and anguish is not in vain.
Nay, the majority of pains may be cured;
When you seek those cures earnestly you find them."
The men of Saba replied, "O men, these pains of ours

Are not of the sort 'that admit of cure.
Long time ye utter these presages and warnings,
But our bonds are made thereby heavier every moment.
If our sickness admitted of a cure,
It would certainly have been lessened by your spells.
When the body is obstructed water reaches not the liver,
Though one drinks the ocean, it passes elsewhere.
Then of course the hands and feet become dropsical,
And. yet that draught does not quench his thirst."
The prophets replied, "To despair is wrong,
The mercy and grace of God are boundless.
One must not despair of the grace of such a Benefactor,
One must cling to the stirrup-straps of God.
Ah! many are the conditions which at first are hard,
But, are afterwards relieved and lose their harshless.
Oftentimes hope succeeds to hopelessness,
Many times does sunlight succeed to darkness.
We admit that ye are weighted as with stones,
_And that ye have locks upon your ears and your hearts. 4
No condition of ours is altogether as we wish,
Our business is to be resigned and to obey.
God has enjoined this servitude upon us;
We say not this merely on our own authority.
We enjoy life on condition of doing His will;
If He bids us, we sow our seed upon the sand.
The soul of the prophet cares for naught but God,
It has naught to do with approving or disapproving His works."
The men of Saba replied, "If ye yourselves are happy,
Ye make us miserable and annoy and disturb us.
Our souls were void of all anxieties,
And ye have plunged us into cares and anxieties.
The comfort and harmony which we enjoyed heretofore
Have been rent in pieces by your evil presages.
We used to be as parrots munching sugar,

Ye have made us as fowls brooding on death.
On every side stories inspiring anxiety,
On every side sounds exciting fears:
On every side in the world an evil presage,
On every side evil portents threatening punishment:
This is the burden of your parables and presages,
This the purport of your awe-inspiring stories."
The prophets replied, "Our evil presages
Are corroborated by the state of your souls.
Suppose you are sleeping in a place of danger,
And serpents are drawing near to bite your heads,
A kind friend will inform you of your danger,
Saying, 'Jump up, lest the serpent devour you.'
You reply, 'Why do you utter evil presages?'
He answers, 'What presage? Up, and see for yourself!
By means of this evil presage I rouse you,
And release you from danger and lead you to your home.'
Like a prophet he warns you of hidden danger,
For a prophet sees what worldlings cannot see."
Mercy inclines the good to devotion, but vengeance the bad.
If you do a kindness to a generous man, 'tis fitting,
For each kindness he will return seven hundredfold.
When you treat a base man with scorn and contumely,
He will become your slave in all sincerity.
Infidels when enjoying prosperity do wrong,
When they are in hell they cry, "O our Lord!"
For base men are purified when they suffer evil,
And when they enjoy prosperity they do evil.
Wherefore the mosque of their devotion is hell,
As the snare is the fetter of wild fowl.
The prison is the hermitage of the wicked thief,
For when he is there he is ever crying to God.
Whereas the object of man's being is to worship God,
Hell is ordained as a place of worship for the proud; 5
Man has the power to engage in any actions soever,

But worship of God is the main object of his existence.
Read the text, 6 "I have not created Jinns and men but to
worship me."
The only object of the world is to worship God.
Though the object of a book is to teach an art,
If you make a pillow of it, it serves that purpose too.
Yet its main object is not to serve as a pillow,
But to impart knowledge and useful instruction.
If you use a sword for a tent-peg,
You prefer the worse use of it to the better.
Though the object of all men's being is wisdom,
Yet each man has a different place of worship.
The place of worship of the noble is nobility,
The place of worship of the base is degradation.
Smite the base to make them bow the head.
Give to the noble to make them repay liberally.
Inasmuch as the base are evil and arrogant,
Hell and humbling are the "small gate" for them.
Verily God has created two places of adoration,
Hell for the base and increased bliss for the noble.
Even so Moses made a small gate in Jerusalem, 7
To make the Israelites bow the head in entering it.
The discussion is continued and illustrated by anecdotes of
the Sufi who preferred a table with no food upon it, because
he ever sought "not-being," of Jacob's vision of Joseph, and of
a devout slave who obtained leave of his master to say his
prayers in a mosque, but tarried there so long that the doors
were shut, and he could not get out, nor his master in. The
prophets at last despaired of making any impression upon the
unbelievers, but called to mind the text "When at last the
Apostles lost all hope, and deemed that they were reckoned
as liars, our aid reached them, and we delivered whom we
would, but our vengeance was not averted from the wicked."
8
The despair of the prophets.

The prophets said, "How long, in our benevolence,
Shall we give to this and that one good advice?
How long shall we hammer cold iron in vain?
How long waste breath in blowing into a lattice?
Men are moved by God's decree and fixed ordinance, 9
As sharp-set teeth are caused by heat of belly.
'Tis Primal Soul that dominates the Second Soul,10
Fish begins to stink at the head, not the tail.
Yet be advised and keep your steed straight as an arrow,
When God says 'Proclaim' we must obey. 11
O men, ye know not to which party ye belong, 12
Exert yourselves then, till ye see which ye are.
When you place goods upon a ship,
You do it in trust that the voyage will be prosperous;
You know not which of the two events will befall you,
Whether you will be drowned or come safe to land.
If you say, 'Till I know which will be my fate
I will not set foot upon the ship;
Shall I be drowned on the voyage or a survivor?
Reveal to me in which class I shall be.
I shall not undertake the voyage on the chance
On the bare hope of reaching land, as the rest do.'
In that case no trade at all will be undertaken by you,
As the secret of these two events is always hidden.
The lamp of the heart, that is a timid trader,
Acquires neither loss nor gain by its ventures.13
Nay, it acquires loss, for it is precluded from gain;
'Tis the lamp that takes fire that acquires light.
Since all things are dependent on probability,
Religion is so first of all, for thereby you find release.
In this world no knocking at the door is possible
Save hope, and God knows what is best."
Probability the guide of life in religion as well as in common
matters. "Religion dependent an hope and fear." 14
The final cause of trading is hope or probability,

When traders work themselves lean as spindles. 15
When the merchant goes to his shop in the morning,
He does so in hope and probability of gaining bread.
If you have no hope of getting bread, why go?
There is the fear of loss, since you are not strong.
But does not this fear of utter loss in your trade
Become weakened in the course of your exertions?
You say, "Although the fear of loss is before me,
Yet I feel greater fear in remaining idle.
I have a better hope through exerting myself;
My fear is increased by remaining idle."
Why then, O faint-hearted one, in the matter of religion
Are you paralysed by the fear of loss?
See you not how the traders in this market of ours
Make large profits, both apostles and saints?
What a mine of wealth awaits them on leaving it,
Seeing they make such profits while still here!
Fire is soft to them as cotton raiment,
The ocean bears them gently like a porter;
Iron in their hands is soft as wax,
The winds are their obedient slaves.

*NOTES:

1. Koran xxxiv. 14.
2. Anvar i Suhaili, chap. iv. Story IV.
3. Koran xxxvi. 6.
4. Koran lxi. 5: "God led their hearts astray."
5. God said, "Come ye either in obedience, or in spite of your wishes" (Koran xli. 10).
6. Koran li. 56.
7. See Koran ii. 55, with Sale's note.
8. Koran xii. 11.
9. "All things have we created after a fixed decree, every action great and small is written." Koran liv. 49.
10. The Logos or first Emanation produced the second or "Universal Soul."

11. "O Apostle! proclaim all that hath been sent down" (Koran v. 71).

12. "Which party," i.e., those doomed to be saved or those doomed to destruction.

13. "Nothing shall be reckoned to a man save that for which he hath made effort" (Koran liii. 40).

14. So Sa'di Bostan Book I. Cp. Butler's Analogy, Conclusion.

15. i.e., exert themselves much.

STORY XIV.
Miracles performed by the Prophet Muhammad.

It is related that the Prophet was once present at a banquet,
and after he had eaten and drunk, his servant Anas threw the
napkin which he had used into the fire, and the napkin was
not burnt, 'but only purified by the fire. On another occasion a
caravan of Arabs was traveling in the desert, and was in sore
distress through lack of water, whereupon the Prophet
miraculously increased the water in a single water-skin, so
that it sufficed to supply the needs of all the travelers.
Moreover, the negro who carried the water-skin was rendered
as white and fair as Joseph. Again, a heathen woman came to
the Prophet carrying her infant, aged only two months, and
the infant saluted the Prophet as the veritable apostle of God.
Again, when the prophet was about to put on his sandals, an
eagle swooped down upon one of them and carried it off,
when a viper was seen to drop from the sandal. The Prophet
was at first inclined to grumble at this stroke of ill-luck; but
when he saw the viper his discontent was turned into
thankfulness to God, who had thus miraculously saved him
from being bitten by the viper.
In difficulties there is provided a way of salvation 1.
In this tale there is a warning for thee, O Soul,
That thou mayest acquiesce in God's ordinances,
And be wary and not doubt God's benevolence,
When sudden misfortunes befall thee.
Let others grow pale from fear of ill fortune,
Do thou smile like the rose at loss and gain;

For the rose, though its petals be torn asunder,
Still smiles on, and it is never cast down.
It says, "Why should I fall into grief in disgrace?
I gather beauty even from the thorn of disgrace."
Whatsoever is lost to thee through God's decree
Know of a surety is so much gained from misfortune.
What is Sufiism? 'Tis to find joy in the heart
Whensoever distress and care assail it.
Know troubles to be that eagle of the Prophet's
Which carried off the sandal of that holy one,
In order to save his foot from the bite of the viper
O excellent device! to preserve him from harm.
'Tis said, "Mourn not for your slaughtered cattle
If a wolf has harried your flocks;"
For that calamity may avert a greater calamity,
And that loss may ward off a more grievous loss.
*NOTES:
1. Freytag, Arabum Proverbia, vol. iii. p. 334.

STORY XV.
The Man who asked Moses to teach him the language of animals.

A certain man came to Moses and desired to be taught the language of animals, for, he said, men used their language only to get food and for purposes of deception, and possibly a knowledge of animals' languages might stimulate his faith. Moses was very unwilling to comply with his request, as he knew such knowledge would prove destructive to him, but, on his persisting, took counsel of God, and finally taught him the language of fowls and dogs. Next morning the man went amongst the fowls, and heard a discussion between the cock and the dog. The dog was abusing the cock for picking up the morsels of bread which fell from their master's table, because the cock could find plenty of grains of corn to eat, whereas the dog could only eat bread. The cock, to appease him, said that on the morrow the master's horse would die, and then the dog would have enough and to spare. The master, hearing this, at once sold his horse, and the dog, being disappointed of his meal, again attacked the cock. The cock then told him the mule would die, whereupon the master sold the mule. Then the cock foretold the death of a slave, and the master again sold the slave. At this the dog, losing patience, upbraided the cock as the chief of deceivers, and the cock excused himself by showing that all three deaths had taken place just as he had predicted, but the master had sold the horse, mule, and slave, and had thrown the loss on others. He added that, to punish him for his fraudulent dealing, the master would himself die on the morrow, and there would be plenty for the dog to eat at the funeral feast. Hearing this, the master went to Moses in

great distress, and prayed to be saved. Moses besought the
Lord for him, and gained permission that he should die in the
peace of God.

Why freewill is good for man.

God said, "Do thou grant his earnest request,
Enlarge his faculty according to his freewill.
Freewill is as the salt to piety,
Otherwise heaven itself were matter of compulsion.
In its revolutions reward and punishment were needless,
For 'tis freewill that has merit at the great reckoning.
If the whole world were framed to praise God,
There would be no merit in praising God.
Place a sword in his hand and remove his impotence,
To see if he turns out a warrior or a robber.
Because freewill is that wherewith 'we honor Adam,' 1
Half the swarm become bees and half wasps.
The faithful yield honeycombs like bees,
The infidels yield store of poison like wasps.
For the faithful feed on choice herbs,
So that, like bees, their chyle yields life-giving food,
Whilst infidels feed on filth and garbage,
And generate poison according to their food."
Men inspired of God are the fountain of life;
Men of delusions are a synonym for death.
In the world the praise "Well done faithful servant!"
Is given to freewill which is used with prudence.
If all dissolute men were shut up in prison,
They would all be temperate and devout and pious.
When power of choice is absent actions are worthless;
But beware lest death snatch away your capital!
Your power of choice is a capital yielding profit,
Remember well the day of final account!
*NOTES:
1. Koran xvii. 72.

STORY XVI.
The Woman who lost all her infants.

A woman bore many children in succession, but none of them
lived beyond the age of three or four months. In great distress
she cried to God, and then beheld in a vision the beautiful
gardens of Paradise, and many fair mansions therein, and
upon one of these mansions she read her own name inscribed.
And a voice from heaven informed her that God would
accept the sorrows she had endured in lieu of her blood shed
in holy war, as, owing to her sex, she was unable to go out to
battle like the men. On looking again, the woman beheld in
Paradise all the children she had lost, and she cried, "O Lord !
they were lost to me, but were safe with Thee!"
This story is followed by anecdotos of Hamza going out to
battle without his coat-of-mail, of the Prophet advising a man
who complained of being cheated in his bargains to take time
before completing them, and of the death of Bilal,
Muhammad's crier, and by illustrations of the illusive nature
of the world, of the difference between things self-evident and
mere matters of inference, and between knowing a thing
through illustrations and on the authority of others and
knowing it as it really is in its essence.
The difference between knowing a thing merely by
similitudes and on the authority of others, and knowing the
very essence thereof.
God's mercy is known through the fruits thereof,
But who save God knows His essence? 1
No one knows the very essence of God's attributes
But only in their effects and by similitudes.
A child knows naught of the nature of sexual intercourse,

Except what you tell him, that it is like sweetmeats.
Yet how far does the pleasure of sexual intercourse
Really resemble that derived from sweetmeats?
Nevertheless the fiction produces a relation
Between you, with your perfect knowledge, and the child;
So that the child knows the matter by a similitude,
Though he knows not its essence or actual nature.
Hence if he says, "I know it," 'tis not far wrong
And if he says, "I know it not," 'tis not wrong.
Should one say, "Do you know Noah,
That prophet of God and luminary of the Spirit?"
If you say, "Do I not know him, for that moon
Is more famed than the sun and moon of heaven?
Little children in their schools,
And elders in their mosques,
All read his name prominently in the Koran,
And preachers tell his story from times of yore;"
You say true, for you know him by report,
Though the real nature of Noah is not revealed to you.
On the other hand, if you say, "What know I of Noah
As his contemporaries knew him?
I am a poor ant what can I know of the elephant?
What knows a fly of the motions of the elephant?"
This statement also is true, O brother,
Seeing that you know not his real nature.
But this impotence to perceive real essence,
Though common to ordinary men, is not universal;
Because essence and its deepest secrets
Are open and manifest to the eyes of the perfect.
Negation and affirmation of one proposition are lawful;
When the aspects differ the relation is double.
"Thou castest not when thou castest" 2 shows such relation,
Here negation and affirmation are both correct.
Thou castest it, since it is in thy hand,
Thou castest not, since 'tis God who affords the strength.

The might of the sons of Adam is limited,
How can a handful of sand shatter an army?
The sand was in man's hands, the casting was God's.
Owing to the two relations negation and affirmation are both true.
The infidels know the prophets,
As well as they doubtless know their own children;
Yea, the infidels know them as well as their own sons,
By a hundred tokens and a hundred evidences,
But from envy and malice conceal their knowledge,
And incline themselves to say, "We know them not."
So when God says in one place "knows them,"
In another He says, "None knows them beside me."
For in truth they are hid under God's overshadowing, 3
And none but God knows them by actual experience.
Therefore take this declaration with its context,
Remembering how you know and do not know Noah.
*NOTES:
1. There is a Hadis, "Think on God's mercies, and not on His essence."
2. Koran viii. 17. Said of the sand cast into the eyes of the men of Mecca at Beder.
3. See Gulshan i Raz, I. 354, where the commentator says the allusion is to Moses at Mount Sinai. Koran vii. 139.

STORY XVII.
The Vakil of the Prince of Bokhara.

The Prince of Bokhara had a Vakil who, through fear of
punishment for an offence he had committed, ran away and
remained concealed in Kuhistan and the desert for the space
of ten years. At the end of that time, being unable to endure
absence from his lord and his home any longer, he
determined to return to Bokhara and throw himself at his
lord's feet, and endure whatever punishment his lord might
be pleased to inflict upon him. His friends did all they could
to dissuade him, assuring him that the Prince's wrath was still
hot against him, and that if he appeared at Bokhara he would
be put to death, or at least imprisoned for the rest of his life.
He replied, "O advisers, be silent, for the force of the love
which is drawing me to Bokhara is stronger than the force of
prudent counsels. When love pulls one way all the wisdom of
Abu Hanifa and Ash-Shafi'i is impotent to withstand it. If it
shall please my lord to slay me, I will yield up my life without
reluctance, for this life of estrangement from him which I am
now leading is the same as death, and release from it will be
eternal happiness. I will return to Bokhara and throw myself
at my lord's feet, and say to him, 'Deal with me as thou wilt,
for I can no longer bear absence from thee, and life or death at
thy hands is all the same to me!'" Accordingly, he journeyed
back to Bokhara, counting the very toils and discomforts of
the road sweet and delightful, because they were steps in his
homeward course. When he reached Bokhara his friends and
relations all warned him not to show himself, as the Prince
was still mindful of his offence and bent on punishing him;
but he replied to them as to his other advisers, that he was

utterly regardless of his life, and was resolved to commit himself to his lord's good pleasure. He then went to the court and threw himself at his lord's feet and swooned away. The Prince, seeing the strong affection borne to him by his repentant servant, conceived a similar affection towards him, and descended from his throne and graciously raised him from the ground, and pardoned his offence. Thus it is that eternal life is gained by utter abandonment of one's own life. When God appears to His ardent lover the lover is absorbed in Him, and not so much as a hair of the lover remains. True lovers are as shadows, and when the sun shines in glory the shadows vanish away. He is a true lover of God to whom God says, "I am thine, and thou art mine!"

In the course of this story, which is narrated at great length, are introduced anecdotes of a lover and his mistress, of the Virgin Mary being visited by the "Blessed Spirit" or Angel Gabriel, 1 of the fatal mosque, of Galen's devotion to carnal learning, of Satan's treachery to the men of Mecca at the battle of Bedr, 2 and of Solomon and the gnat. There also occur comments on various texts, and a curious comparison of the trials and wholesome afflictions of the righteous to the boiling of potherbs in a saucepan by the cook.

The reply of the lover when asked by his mistress which city of all those he had seen was most pleasing in his sight.

A damsel said to her lover, "O fond youth,
You have visited many cities in your travels;
Which of those cities seems most delightful to you?"
He made answer, "The city wherein my love dwells.
In whatever nook my queen alights,
Though it be as the eye of a needle, 'tis a wide plain;
Wherever her Yusuf-like face shines as a moon,
Though it be the bottom of a well, 'tis Paradise.
With thee, my love, hell itself were heaven,

With thee a prison would be a rose-garden.
With thee hell would be a mansion of delight,
Without thee lilies and roses would be as flames of fire!"
The answer of the Vakil to those who advised him not to
court death by yielding himself up to his lord.
He said, "I am a drawer of water; water attracts me,
Even though I know water may be my death.
No drawer of water flees from water,
Even though it may cause him a hundred deaths.
Though it may make my hand and belly dropsical,
My love for water will never be lessened.
I should say, when they asked me about my belly,
'Would that the ocean might flow into it!'
Though the bottle of my belly were burst with water,
And though I should die, my death would be acceptable.
Wheresoever I see one seeking water, I envy him,
And cry, 'Would I were in his place!'
My hand is a tabor and my belly a drum,
Like the rose I beat the drum of love of water.
Like the earth or like a fetus I devour blood,
Since I became a lover this is my occupation.
If that 'Faithful Spirit' should shed my blood,
I would drink it up drop by drop like the earth.
At night I boil on the fire like a cooking-pot,
From morn till eve I drink blood like the sand.
It repents me that I planned a stratagem,
And that I fled from before his wrath.
Tell him to sate his wrath on my poor life,
He is the 'Feast of Sacrifice,' and I his loving cow. 3
The cow, whether it eats or sleeps,
Thinks of naught but sacrificing itself.
Know me to be that cow of Moses which gave its life,
Each part of me gives life to the righteous.
That cow of Moses was made a sacrifice,
And its least part became a source of life.

That murdered man leapt up from his deadness
At the words, ' Strike the corpse with part of her.' 4
O pious ones, slay the cow (of lust),
If ye desire true life of soul and spirit!
I died as inanimate matter and arose a plant,
I died as a plant and rose again an animal. 5
I died as an animal and arose a man.
Why then should I fear to become less by dying?
I shall die once again as a man
To rise an angel perfect from head to foot!
Again when I suffer dissolution as an angel,
I shall become what passes the conception of man!
Let me then become non-existent, for non-existence
Sings to me in organ tones, 'To him shall we return.' 6
Know death to be the gathering together of the people.
The water of life is hidden in the land of darkness.
Like a water-lily seek life there!
Yea, like that drawer of water, at the risk of life,
Water will be his death, yet he still seeks water,
And still drinks on, and God knows what is right.
O lover, cold-hearted and void of loyalty,
Who from fear for your life shun the beloved!
O base one, behold a hundred thousand souls
Dancing towards the deadly sword of his love:
Behold water in a pitcher; pour it out;
Will that water run away from the stream?
When that water joins the water of the stream
It is lost therein, and becomes itself the stream.
Its individuality is lost, but its essence remains,
And hereby it becomes not less nor inferior.
I will hang myself upon my lord's palm-tree
In excuse for having fled away from him!"
Even as a ball rolling along on head and face,
He fell at the feet of the Prince with streaming eyes.
The people were all on the alert, expecting

That the Prince would burn him or hang him,
Saying, "Moth-like he has seen the blaze of the light,
And fool-like has plunged therein and lost his life."
But the torch of love is not like that torch,
'Tis light, light in the midst of light,
'Tis the reverse of torches of fire,
It appears to be fire, but is all sweetness.
Love generates love. "If ye love God, God will love you" 7
That. Bokharian then cast himself into the flame,
But his love made the pain endurable;
And as his burning sighs ascended to heaven,
The love of the Prince was kindled towards him.
The heart of man is like the root of a tree,
Therefrom grow the leaves on firm branches. 8
Corresponding to that root grow up branches
As well on the tree as on souls and intellects.
The tops of the perfect trees reach the heavens,
The roots firm, and the branches in the sky.
Since then the tree of love has grown up to heaven,
How shall it not also grow in the heart of the Prince?
A wave washes away the remembrance of the sin from his heart,
For from each heart is a window to other hearts.
Since in each heart there is a window to other hearts,
They are not, separated and shut off like two bodies.
Thus, even though two lamp-dishes be not joined,
Yet their light is united in a single ray.
No lover ever seeks union with his beloved,
But his beloved is also seeking union with him.
But the lover's love makes his body lean,
While the beloved's love makes hers fair and lusty.
When in this heart the lightning spark of love arises,
Be sure this love is reciprocated in that heart.
When the love of God arises in thy heart,
Without doubt God also feels love for thee.

The noise of clapping of hands is never heard
From one of thy hands unaided by the other hand
The man athirst cries, "Where is delicious water?"
Water too cries, "Where is the water-drinker?"
This thirst in my soul is the attraction of the water;
I am the water's and the water is mine.
God's wisdom in His eternal foreknowledge and decree
Made us to be lovers one of the other.
Nay more, all the parts of the world by this decree
Are arranged in pairs, and each loves its mate.
Every part of the world desires its mate,
Just as amber attracts blades of straw.
Heaven says to earth, "All hail to thee!
We are related to one another as iron and magnet."
Heaven is man and earth woman in character;
Whatever heaven sends it, earth cherishes.
When earth lacks heat, heaven sends heat;
When it lacks moisture and dew, heaven sends them.
The earthy sign 9 succours the terrestrial earth,
The watery sign (Aquarius) sends moisture to it;
The windy sign sends the clouds to it,
To draw off unwholesome exhalations.
The fiery sign (Leo) sends forth the heat of the sun,
Like a dish heated red-hot in front and behind.
The heaven is busily toiling through ages,
Just as men labor to provide food for women.
And the earth does the woman's work, and toils
In bearing offspring and suckling them.
Know then earth and heaven are endued with sense,
Since they act like persons endued with sense.
If these two lovers did not suck nutriment from each other,
Why should they creep together like man and wife?
Without the earth how could roses and saffron grow?
For naught can grow from the sole heat and rain of heaven.
This is the cause of the female seeking the male,

That the work of each may be accomplished.
God has instilled mutual love into man and woman,
That the world may be perpetuated by their union.
Earth says to the earth of the body, "Come away,
Quit the soul and come to me as dust.
Thou art of my genus, and wilt be better with me,
'Thou had'st better quit the soul and fly to me!"
Body replies "True, but my feet are fast bound,
Though like thee I suffer from separation."
Water calls out to the moisture of the body,
"O moisture, return to me from your foreign abode!"
Fire also calls out to the heat of the body,
"Thou art of fire; return to thy root!"
In the body there are seventy-and-two diseases;
It is ill compacted owing to the struggle of its elements.
Disease comes to rend the body asunder,
And to drag apart its constituent elements.
The four elements are as birds tied together by the feet;
Death, sickness and disease loose their feet asunder.
The moment their feet are loosed from the others,
'The bird of each element flies off by itself.
The repulsion of each of these principles and causes
Inflicts every moment a fresh pang on our bodies.
That it may dissolve these composite bodies of ours,
The bird of each part tries to fly away to its origin;
But the wisdom of God prevents this speedy end,
And preserves their union till the appointed day.
He says, "O parts, the appointed time is not yet;
It is useless for you to take wing before that day."
But as each part desires reunion with its original,
How is it with the soul who is a stranger in exile?
It says, "O parts of my habitation here below,
My absence is sadder than yours, as I am heaven-born.
The body loves green pastures and running water,
For this cause that its origin is from them.

The love of the soul is for life and the living one,
Because its origin is the Soul not bound to place.
The love of the soul is for wisdom and knowledge,
That of the body for houses, gardens, and vineyards;
The love of the soul is for things exalted on high,
That of the body for acquisition of goods and food.
The love too of Him on high is directed to the soul:
Know this for 'He loves them that love Him.'" 10
The sum is this, that whoso seeks another,
The soul of that other who is sought inclines to him.
Let us quit the subject. Love for that soul athirst
Was kindled in the breast of the Prince of Bokhara.
The smoke of that love and the grief of that burning heart
Ascended to his master and excited his compassion.
The praises addressed to the Prince by the Vakil.

He said, "O phoenix of God and goal of the spirit
I thank thee that thou hast come back from Mount Qaf!
O Israfil of the resurrection-day of love,
O love, love, and heart's desire of love!
Let thy first boon to me be this,
To lend thine ear to my orisons.
Though thou knowest my condition clearly,
O protector of slaves, listen to my speech.
A thousand times, O prince incomparable,
Has my reason taken flight in desire to see thee,
And to hear thee and to listen to thy words,
And to behold thy life-giving smiles.
Thy inclining thine ear to my supplications
Is as a caress to my misguided soul.
The baseness of my heart's coin is known to thee,
But thou hast accepted it as genuine coin.
Thou art proud towards the arrogant and proud;
All clemencies are as naught to thy clemency.

First hear this, that while I remained in absence,
First and last alike escaped me.
Secondly, hear this. O prince beloved,
That I searched much, but found no second to thee.
Thirdly, that when I had departed outside thee,
I said it was like the Christian Trinity. 11
Fourthly, when my harvest was burned up,
I knew not the fourth from the fifth.
Wheresoever thou findest blood on the roads,
Trace it, and 'tis tears of blood from my eyes.
My words are thunder, and these sighs and tears
Are drawn by it as rain from the clouds.
I am distracted between speaking and weeping.
Shall I weep, or shall I speak, or what shall I do?
If I speak, my weeping ceases;
If I weep, I cease to praise and magnify thee."
He spoke thus, and then fell to weeping,
So that high and low wept with him.
So many "Ahs" and "Alases" proceeded from his heart,
That the people of Bokhara formed a circle round him.
Talking sadly, weeping sadly, smiling sadly,
Men and women, small and great, were all assembled.
The whole city wept in concert with him;
Men and women mingled together as on the last day.
Then Heaven said to Earth,
"If you never saw a resurrection-day, see it here!"
Reason was amazed, saying, "What love, what ecstasy!
Is his separation more wondrous, or his reunion?"
*NOTES:
1. Koran xix. 18.
2. Koran viii. 10.
3. The Id ul Azha, or the Feast of Sacrifices, held on the tenth
day of the month Zul Hijja. It is also called "The Cow
Festival."
4. This refers to Koran ii. 63. The cow was to be sacrificed in

63

order that a murderer might be discovered by striking the corpse with a piece of her flesh.

5. i.e., Earth losing its own form becomes vegetable, vegetable again perishes to feed and be transmuted into animal, , and in like manner animal becomes man. See the passage of Milton quoted below, and Gulshan i Raz, I. 490 and note.

6. Koran ii. 153: "Verily we are God's, and to Him shall we return."

7. Koran iii. 29.

8. "Seest thou not to what God likeneth a good word? To a good tree, its root firmly fixed, and its branches in the heaven" (Koran xiv. 29).

9. i.e., of the zodiac.

10. Koran v. 59.

11. "They surely are infidels who say, 'God is the third of three,' for there is no God but one God" (Koran v. 77).

STORY XVIII.
The Deadly Mosque.

In the suburbs of a certain city there was a mosque in which none could sleep a night and live. Some said it was haunted by malevolent fairies; others, that it was under the baneful influence of a magic spell; some proposed to put up a notice warning people not to sleep there, and others advised that the door should be kept locked. At last a stranger came to that city and desired to sleep in the mosque, saying that he did not fear to risk his life, as the life of the body was naught, and God has said, "Wish for death if you are sincere." 1 The men of the city warned him again and again of the danger, and rebuked him for his foolhardiness, reminding him that not improbably Satan was tempting him to his own destruction, as he tempted the men of Mecca at the battle of Bedr. 2 The stranger, however, would not be dissuaded, but persisted in his purpose of sleeping in the mosque. He said that he was as one of the devoted agents of the Ismailians, who were always ready to sacrifice their lives at the bidding of their chiefs, and that the terrors of death did not appal him any more than the noise of a little drum beaten by a boy to scare away birds could appal the great drum-bearing camel that used to march at the head of King Mahmud's army. Accordingly, he slept in the mosque, and at midnight he was awakened by a terrible voice, as of one about to attack him. But instead of being dismayed, he bethought himself of the text "Assault them with thy horsemen and thy footmen," 3 and confronted his unseen foe, challenging him to show himself and stand to his arms. At these words the spell was dissipated, and showers of gold fell on all sides, which the brave hero proceeded to appropriate.

The "knowledge of certainty" and the "eye of certainty".
Our body and substance are snow, doomed to perish,
God is He who buys them, for "God hath bought them." 4
You prefer this perishing snow to God's price
Because you are in doubt and have not certainty;
And, strange to say, opinion abides in you, O weak one,
And never flies away to the garden of certainty.
Every opinion is aiming at certainty, O son,
And more and more moves its wings towards certainty.
When it reaches knowledge it stands erect,
And its knowledge again hastes on towards certainty,
Because in the approved road of the faith
Knowledge is lower than certainty, but above opinion.
Know knowledge aspires to certainty,
And certainty again to sight and ocular evidence.
In the chapter, "Desire of riches occupieth you," 5
After "Nay," read "Would that ye knew!"
Knowledge conducts you to sight, O knower!
"If ye are certain, ye shall see hell-fire."
Sight follows on certainty with no interval,
Just as reasoned knowledge is born of opinion.
See the account of this in the chapter cited,
How knowledge of certainty becomes the eye of certainty.
As for me, I am above both opinion and certainty;
My head is not affected by your cavils.
Since my mouth has eaten of His sweetmeats,
I am become clear-sighted, and see him face to face!
The righteous are exposed to trials for their improvement, as
potherbs are boiled to make them fit for food.

Behold these potherbs boiling in the pot,
How they jump and toss about in the heat of the fire.
Whilst they are boiling, they keep leaping up,

Even to the top of the pot, and utter cries,
Saying to the housewife, "Why do you set us on the fire?
Now you have bought us, why should you afflict us?"
The housewife pushes them down with her spoon, saying,
"Be still, and boil well, and leap not off the fire.
I do not boil you because I dislike you,
But that you may acquire a good savor and taste.
When you become food you will be mingled with life;
This trial is not imposed on you to distress you.
In the garden you drank water soft and fresh;
That water-fed one was reserved for this fire.
Mercy was first shown to it before vengeance,
That mercy might train it to be proof against trial;
Mercy was shown to it previously to vengeance,
That it might acquire its substance of being.
Because flesh and skin grow not without tender care,
How should they not grow when warmed by the Friend's
love.
If vengeance follows as a necessary consequence,
That you may make an offering of that substance,
Mercy follows again to compensate for it,
That you may be purified and raised above your nature.
I am Abraham, and you his son under the knife.
Lay down your head! 'I have seen I must sacrifice you.' 6
Yield your head to vengeance, your heart to constancy,
That I may cut your throat like an Ismailian's.
I cut off your head, but that head is such
That it is restored to life by being cut off!"
My main object herein is to inculcate resignation,
O Mosalman! it behoves you to seek resignation. 7
O potherbs, you boil in trials and sufferings
That neither existence nor self may remain in you.
Though you once smiled in that earthly garden,
You are really roses of the garden of life and sight.
If you are torn away from the garden of earth,

You become sweet food to revive man's life;
Yea, become his food and strength and thought! 8
You were only milk, you become a lion of the forest!
You issue from God's attributes at first;
Return again back to those attributes with all speed!
You come from the clouds and sunshine and sky,
Then assume moral qualities and ascend the sky.
You come in the form of rain and sunshine,
You depart endued with excellent attributes.
You begin as a part of the sun, clouds, and stars,
You rise to be breath, act, word, and thought!
The life of animals comes from the death of plants.
True is the saying, 'Kill me, O faithful ones!'
Since such exaltation awaits us after death.
True it is that 'In our death is life.'
Acts, words, and faith are the food of the King,
So that in this ascent one attains to heaven.
Thus, as potherbs become the food of men,
They rise above the grade of minerals to that of animals.
Objections of fools to the Masnavi.
A certain goose pops his head out of his coop,
And displays himself as a critic of the Masnavi,
Saying, "This poem, the Masnavi, is childish;
'Tis but a story of the prophets, and so on.
'Tis not an account of the arguments and deep mysteries,
Whereto holy men direct their attention;
Concerning asceticism, and so on to self-annihilation,
Step by step, up to communion with God;
An explanation and definition of each several state,
Whereto the men of heart ascend in their flight."
Whereas the Book of God resembles the Masnavi in this,
The infidels abused it, in the same manner,
Saying, 'It contains old tales and stories; 9
There is no deep analysis or lofty investigation therein.
Little boys can understand it;

It only contains commands and prohibitions,
Accounts of Yusuf and his curled locks,
Accounts of Jacob, of Zulaikha and her love,
Accounts of Adam, of the wheat, and of the serpent Iblis,
Accounts of Hud, of Noah, of Abraham, and the, fire."
Know the words of the Koran are simple,
But within the outward sense is an inner secret one. 10
Beneath that secret meaning is a third,
Whereat the highest wit is dumbfounded.
The fourth meaning has been seen by none
Save God, the Incomparable and All-sufficient.
Thus they go on, even to seven meanings, one by one,
According to the saying of the Prophet, without doubt.
Do thou, O son, confine not thy view to the outward
meaning,
Even as the demons saw in Adam only clay. 11
The outward meaning of the Koran is like Adam's body,
For its semblance is visible, but its soul is hidden.
O reviling dog! thou makest a clamour,
Thou makest thy abuse of the Koran thy destruction. 12
This is not a lion, wherefrom thou canst save thy life,
Or canst secure thyself from his talons!
The Koran cries out even to the last day,
"O people, given up as a prey to ignorance,
If ye have imagined me to be only empty fables,
Ye have sown the seed of reviling and infidelity.
Ye yourselves who abuse me will see yourselves
Annihilated, and made like a tale that is told!"
Solomon and the gnat.
A gnat came in from the garden and fields,
And called on Solomon for justice,
Saying, "O Solomon, you extend your equity
Over demons and the sons of Adam and fairies.
Fish and fowl dwell under the shelter of your justice;
Where is the oppressed one whom your mercy has not

sought?
Grant me redress, for I am much afflicted,
Being cut off from my garden and meadow haunts."
Then Solomon replied, "O seeker of redress,
Tell me from whom do you desire redress?
Who is the oppressor, who, puffed up with arrogance
Has oppressed you and smitten your face?"
The gnat replied, "He from whom I seek redress is the Wind,
'Tis he who has emitted the smoke of oppression at me;
Through his oppression I am in a grievous strait,
Through him I drink blood with parched lip!"
Solomon replied to him, "O sweet voiced one,
You must hear the command of God with all your heart.
God has commanded me saying, 'O dispenser of justice,
Never hear one party without the other!'
Till both parties come into the presence,
The truth is never made plain to the judge."
When the Wind heard the summons, it came swiftly,
And the gnat instantly took flight.
In like manner the seekers of God's presence-seat,
When God appears, those seekers vanish.
Though that union is life eternal,
Yet at first that life is annihilation.

End of the book.

www.ingramcontent.com/pod-product-compliance
Lightning Source LLC
Chambersburg PA
CBHW060000300526
45794CB00003B/1021